JACK THE RIPPER

Leather Apron

THE HISTORY HOUR

CONTENTS

❧ I ☙

INTRODUCTION

❦

Where would we be without Jack the Ripper? More than one hundred years after the unidentified killer ended his crime wave interest in his story remains immense. Strong enough to merit numerous walking tours around London's East End, plus a well-trodden museum popular with tourists and locals alike. Public interest in him has, if anything, grown over time rather than faded into the fog of our memories.

❦

Hundreds of books have been published on his actions, many seeking to provide the definitive truth about who the killer was, from a member of the Royal Family to aristocrat, wealthy industrialist and on to common cutthroat. A catalog of films exists about him. For example, that master of the mysterious and High Priest of Horror, Alfred Hitchcock, based his early 1927 piece, The Lodger: A Story of a London Fog, on the Ripper story.

***

Documentaries, magazine articles and so forth are still written. This book, we hope, will be different to most. It is not going to try to name the killer; to do so would be mere speculation. Instead, we will cover the major aspects of his actions and try to identify the reasons behind them. We will consider some of the most common suspects, and one or two of the less well-known ones. Who knows, by the law of averages and the millions of hours that have been put in by authors, investigators and criminal historians across the globe, there is a fair chance we may hit upon the culprit.

***

If we do, though, we will not know it!

***

We will also seek to give proper time to the victims of the Ripper's crimes; in Victorian England women, unless they were the Queen, counted for little, and the story of the Ripper dwarfs the tales of those he killed. That is not right, even if it was (back then) more understandable. Most of all we will seek to strip away the myth surrounding this appalling man and put his vicious crimes in the context they deserve.

***

Today, the Ripper holds our interests, sends a pleasant chill down our spines, raises a question in our minds. But back in the 1880s, he was viewed differently. The mythology surrounding the man mattered more than his identity. He symbolized all that was wrong with a Victorian Society whose mannered exterior, the dominant force in the world, covered a rats' nest of depravity, exploitation, and discrimination.

۞

While the man himself is mired in myth, there is no doubt that his crimes existed; more likely than not he had five victims – Mary Anne Nicholls, Annie Chapman, Elizabeth Stride, Catherine Eddowes and Mary Jane Kelly – but he could have killed more. Further to this, there may have been more than one Ripper; his fame echoed in a series of copycat crimes. As we read on, we will discover whether Jack the Ripper was simply a vicious killer, or whether he was more, a symbol of his time.

❧ II ☙

JACK THE RIPPER: THE STUFF OF NIGHTMARES OR THE SWEETEST DREAMS?

"Fear is a hungry beast. The more you feed it, the more it grows."

— Kerri Maniscalco, Stalking Jack the Ripper

⚜

We start our story not in the pubs of Whitechapel, nor under the dank archways of Spitalfields nor even on the morticians' slabs. But in the history books.

⚜

To understand the Ripper, we have to understand the society that created him. Ours is the London of Dickens, full of rich men making their fortune on the backs of others, of child labor and workhouses. The fantasy world of Mary Poppins, an Edwardian paradise only twenty years away, could not be further than the truth.

⚜

Chimney sweeps were not chirpy chaps with a winning smile and a nice line in Cockney songs; instead, they were children, paid a pittance, many of who died in the soot-filled chambers into which they were stuffed. If they survived to adulthood, their lungs would be permanently damaged by the detritus they had inhaled.

⚜

Women of the street were not tough-talking, down to earth types with a heart of gold, but instead women who sold their bodies for the price of a stale loaf of bread. Who were constantly at threat from violence and whose disease riddled bodies rarely reached old, or even middle, age.

⚜

In that foggy, dirty, stinking and cramped East End immigrants were abused, refused work and beaten up. It was no wonder that ghettos formed. Drinking was more than a past time; it was a way of life. Many lived in casual houses, or lodgings, where a bed for the night could only be secured with cash up front, and the supervisor would kick you out into the dark – man or woman – if it had been a bad day and you had no money. Often, your choice existed between eating and sleeping under cover, in the relative safety of a dirty room or dormitory.

⚜

With work for women hard to find, many were forced to use the only resource they had, their bodies. Despite the Victorian Britain of romantic fiction, this was a time of hell for the poor.

VICTORIANS – THE
MORAL ONES?

⚜

The future Queen Victoria was born into an age of Royal lasciviousness. Princes were lecherous, kings lewd. They could be, so they were. There was no one to tell them to stop and if the apex of society is corrupted, that creeping rust seeps into lower ramparts. When Victoria became Queen, she was determined to put a stop to this. It was only through chance that she had even ascended to the throne; a mixture of unexpected deaths and lack of heirs pushing her to the top of the line of succession. But now she was there; she was determined to make her mark.

⚜

Her domineering mother, the Duchess of Kent, and her probable lover, the odious Sir John Conroy saw the chance for personal advancement. Together, they devised the Kensington System, in effect a screen that controlled every aspect of the young girl's life and subjected her to frightening levels of queenly instruction. She even slept in the same bedroom as her mother every night until she acquired the throne (at which point her mother was pointedly given her quarters, and the deceitful Conroy received his marching orders.)

๑๙๓

Her marriage to Albert was one of love, not convenience, which was a rarity for the monarchy. The two were inseparable. They were a perfect family, loving towards each other and interested in their wider role as leaders of not only a country but the biggest Empire in the world. And if the King and Queen acted with propriety and decorum then so should the rest of society.

๑๙๓

Out went sexual deviancy, lewdness, misappropriation, and corruption. Except, of course, it didn't. The aristocracy had enjoyed too many years of sinful joys to give them up overnight. The new middle class, that many-layered strata of Victorian society, aspired to be considered on a par with their aristocratic – if often financially poorer – superiors. The working classes in their dirty streets or impoverished villages might still engage in nefarious activities of all kinds, but they were working class and so didn't matter.

๑๙๓

After all, if any urchin or lay about caused trouble they could always be sent to one of the new colonies – Australia being a particularly remote and inhospitable alternative. Failing that, the gallows served the twin purpose of ridding society of its most odious members and entertaining the remainder at the same time.

❧

The truth though was startling different from the pretense. Syphilis remained the rich man's plague, a disease hidden beneath the light; maids became mothers to the sons of their masters and might, if they were lucky, still retain their jobs. Corruption was as rife as ever, sexual deviancy as common. It was just that now, under the new world of Victoria, they happened less overtly. Those Victorians of middle and aristocratic classes learned how to do their worse behind closed doors, instead of in the open.

❧

Hidden by the cloak of religious piety, appalling acts of savagery were happening in India, under the auspices of the East India Company and in the name of Britain. Industrialization made millionaires of some but martyred many more into absolute destitution. A walk through the stinking, crime-ridden streets of Britain's major cities told a far truer story than well-dressed men in monocles and top hats in Jermyn Street.

❧

The world and the working classes had to witness the pomp and propriety of the British man. Not their sordid reality. It was what Victoria expected. And so that twin world continued; as perverse as ever when out of sight, a shining example of to what the human race could aspire when on a show.

Then, in late 1861, Victoria's eldest son, Prince Albert Edward, Prince of Wales – Bertie to his friends – committed one outrageous act of too many. Bertie's genes, it seemed, were too closely tied to his ancestors' blood, and gambling, drinking, merry and lovemaking were all far too transparent parts of his character. Prince Albert headed to Cambridge to offer a few words of fatherly wisdom.

He took his son for a lengthy walk in the rain and, happy that the boy had learned his lesson, headed back to Windsor. There, within days, he had contracted an infection which rapidly turned to typhoid, and a couple of weeks later, he was dead.

Victoria was devastated and blamed her eldest son. She spent the rest of her life in black (although maybe not, it should be said, when engaging in regular spells of hot sport with her lover, the Scotsman John Brown). For many years she effectively disappeared from public life. While that made things tricky for politicians – the monarch still had a substantial say in political matters and Victoria was opinionated, if private – it meant that those excesses of spirit which had been hidden for years behind the front of Victorian values could now become more open in their lechery. And the working classes, in their slums, were not happy.

Meanwhile, a further event became a cause of unrest, specifically in the streets of East London. Anti-Semitism in Europe was on the crest of one of its far too frequent waves. Life for Jews in Russia, Poland and Germany was extremely difficult, and a wave of immigration hit the East End the cramped, dirty streets of Spitalfields and Whitechapel. By 1888, the year of the Ripper, estimates put the number of Jews in these areas at around 50000.

But if a persecuted people had left their homes in search of a better life, they did not find it in London's East End. Not only were homes overcrowded and hard to come by, but so were jobs. There were enough of these – the Thames being a major world port at the time - but nationalism was rife. If the toffs hid their physical depravities in the metaphorical closet, then the poor shut their jingoistic ones in there too. Britain had an empire, Britain led the world. OK, so the streets around St. Mary Matfelon might not be paved with gold (or silver for that matter) but the people were British, and that made them superior to foreigners. Especially Jewish ones.

Anti-Semitism might take the form of horrendous caricature in the publications of Charles Dickens (consider, for example, Fagin) but they took a more direct form in Whitechapel. Jews could not find work. If they did get a job, they would be treated so aggressively and abusively that their lives might depend on them giving it up.

So not only were Jews aliens in the East End, but they were the poorest ones, ones who needed to seek other ways of earning a living. The Pall Mall Gazette (the first '*tabloid*' newspaper) told its readers in 1886,

> 'the foreign Jews of no nationality whatever are
> becoming a pest and a menace to the poor, native
> East Londoner.'

That right wing rag would soon change its tune.

☙❧

A third factor led to the creation of the myth of Jack the Ripper. This was closely connected to the back-garden indulgences of the rich, as well as the need to provide cheap entertainment to a local population with little to keep them occupied. Beyond drinking. And fighting.

☙❧

In the wealthy West End of London (which, by the way, was also a hotbed of crime and prostitution), the great new theaters – the Lyric, Drury Lane and so on – were providing entertainment to those who could afford it. The East End got its own, somewhat cheaper, alternative. The Music Hall. A place that offered more than just musical fun.

☙❧

Let's be clear; we are not talking here about the highbrow establishments of Charing Cross Road or Shaftesbury Avenue; nor even the suburban establishments in the expanding city. The music halls of Whitechapel and Spitalfields were much more earthy institutions. Entry was cheap, but the owners knew how to pack their audience in. Two shows a night, both full to bursting.

In the stalls, the audience would usually stand, like penny stinkers at Shakespeare's Globe. But upstairs, in the circle, the hats would be smarter than the potted versions worn by the vocal youths below. Here, the show would be watched by the well dressed, the smart, the industrialists and professionals and, occasionally, even by the aristocracy.

But why? These people were quite capable of paying West End prices, and a carriage to one of the new theaters was a far safer prospect than hustling through the dark and dank streets of the East End. But those expensive establishments lacked something this lowest class of entertainment offered. Because if Lord So and So or Sir This or That was taken by the performance of a certain dancer or even a promising young male comedian, then a quiet word in an usher's ear would deliver that nubile young thing to the rich man after the show.

What then took place would stay behind the fog of Victorian propriety; we do not have to think too hard to draw an accurate picture of the sordid scenes that would ensue.

And that is Victorian Britain. Everybody knew what these rich gents, fat on the proceeds of their good fortune, were up to - but nobody admitted it. Which, in turn, provoked an enormous amount of fury among the working-class men of the time. It was bad enough being walked upon, but to have those with money exploiting them further was too much to take.

❧

Their anger, bubbling under like a volcano about to erupt, would come to the fore when the Ripper began to strike.

❧

Because it offered a very plausible chance that the Ripper was a man of means.

❧ III ❧
THE COVETOUS SUSPECT

"I was determined to be both pretty and fierce, as Mother had said I could be. Just because I was interested in a man's job didn't mean I had to give up being girly. Who defined those roles anyhow?"

— Kerri Maniscalco, Stalking Jack the Ripper

A MODERN DAY PROFILE

※※※

Whatever the reason, Jack the Ripper has and continues, to hold the fascination of people across the world. And that is not just the general public, but law enforcement organizations as well. Included among these is the FBI. They have produced a psychological profile of the killer, and conclude the following:

- The killer was white and male;
- He lived in, or close to the Whitechapel area of East London;
- He was aged between twenty-eight and thirty-six years of age;
- His violent nature was one that he could experience legitimately within his workplace, suggesting something like a doctor or police officer;
- He lacked a significant father figure in his childhood;

- He had some kind of physical or psychological defect which caused anger;
- He most probably stopped killing because he was either caught for some other crime, or the risk of capture became too great. The second alternative suggests somebody in control of his tendencies.

This profile gives us a chance to judge suspects against some fixed criteria.

KILLING FROM JEALOUSY –
JOSEPH BARNETT

❦

Barnett was not a suspect until relatively recently. In the 1970s private investigator, Bruce Paley introduced Barnett as a serious contender for the Ripper title. The idea floated for a few years, Paul Harrison (author of Jack the Ripper: ***The Mystery Solved***) made the case that Barnett could be the killer, but his book is not generally seen as a reliable source of information since its research was considered flawed.

❦

However, in Jack the Ripper: The Simple Truth Paley himself published the reasons behind his suspicion that Joseph Barnett was the serial killer. The book was a culmination of more than a decade of thorough research which makes it well regarded among Ripper aficionados. Let us consider the facts, as we know them, and decide for ourselves whether Paley is correct.

⁂

Barnett worked at Billingsgate Market as a fish porter. Not a job many would choose to do if other opportunities presented themselves. The market itself drew different descriptions depending on how romantic the writer might be. Variously, it was

> 'held within the precincts of a picturesque red brick building...'

(according, at least, to Cruchley's London in 1865); it was a savior for rich and poor alike, as costermongers separated fish by its quality, boxes '*designed for St. James' or St. Giles*','or to be piled onto the costermongers wagons and sold to the East End's fish shops, or traded straight from the middle man (that nugget was written by the chillingly named Dr. Andrew Winter). Perhaps Nathaniel Hawthorne, in his manuscript '*The English Note-Books*' of 1857 was most realistic.

> '...a dirty, evil-smelling, crowded precinct...we had to elbow our way among rough men and slatternly women...'

was the Billingsgate he described.

⁂

And so Barnett is born on 25th May 1858, in London's crowded, insanitary East End and grows up in Whitechapel, London. He is the fourth of five children to John and Catherine Barnett, who had emigrated to London from their Irish home. John worked on the docks of the Thames; hard, unrelenting labor which offered little financial reward for the outlay in time and effort. Later, he became a fish porter.

☙❧

Joseph Barnett was just six years old when his father died of pleurisy in July 1964. His mother seems to disappear without a trace from that point onwards, whether she died or ran off, we don't know, but by the 1871 census, thirteen-year-old Joseph is living in a desperately poor, slum-like ghetto in the evocatively named Spitalfields. His elder brother Daniel, just twenty, is listed as the head of the family.

☙❧

It is a desperately harsh start to life, but one very typical of the inhabitants of this poor part of London during the times of Queen Victoria. The divide between rich and poor in industrial Britain was as marked as it was in most of the undeveloped parts of the world.

☙❧

All four of the boys in the family became fish porters, following in their father's footsteps. Work must have been uncertain because Barnett's description of his role varied between laborer and dock hand as well as a fish porter.

☙❧

As Joseph Barnett entered adulthood, he was already no stranger to drink, (nor depravation and poverty). Indeed, it was in an inn that he met Mary Jane Kelly, who would later become the last (most probably) of the Ripper's victims.

They decided to live together, and Barnett found lodgings in a slum room in George St (apparently, he was '*known*' there, whatever that might mean). They stayed nowhere for long; payment of rent was difficult, and drunkenness added to their problems.

※

Just before the first Ripper killing, he lost his job at the market – supposedly for theft. If Barnett is the Ripper, then this the first of some motives he had for his crimes. Perhaps the loss of his income, and all the associated risk – losing his home, not being able to afford food, heating of clothing – pushed him over the edge.

※

It also led to a further problem. Barnett dreamed of earning enough money to enable Mary to leave behind her life as a prostitute. But the loss of his job put an end to that hope. For her part, Mary seemed to accept her lot and showed no overwhelming desire to cease her trade. Perhaps that said something about their relationship. For all his manifold faults, Barnett loved Mary Kelly; she was fond of him, but no more. Barnett was furious that she was prepared to continue with her life as a prostitute, despite the fear she had of falling victim to whoever was killing her peers. Unable to persuade her to stop her prostitution, he left her.

※

However, according to his statement to the police, the couple remained on good terms and saw each other still. Indeed, according to Barnett, they separated on 30th October 1888 and saw each other (for the final time) on the 8th November, when he visited her at her home to apologize for not having work. According to Barnett, he left her because she had taken in a prostitute to which (as such an upstanding member of Victorian Society) he objected. It is interesting to note that at no time did he tell police that his former lover was herself a prostitute.

❦

From the benefit of hindsight, we can see two more motives for Barnett to embark on his killing spree. Was it possible that he killed the first four prostitutes in an attempt to scare Mary into stopping her trade? And when that failed, did he finally lose the last remnants of control and kill her in the most savage and fevered manner of any of the murders?

❦

During his interview police noted that he stuttered a lot and seemed confused. He repeated words said to him in a strange manner. Could this be nerves? If so, normal nerves of a man facing police interrogation, or the nerves of a person with something to hide? With today's perspective, that behavior might mean he suffered from echolalia, a psychological condition that causes sufferers to repeat phrases automatically. It is an illness that is often seen as a symptom of autism.

❦

Beyond motive, there are some other reasons; some linked to the FBI profile of the killer, which might identify Barnett as the true Jack the Ripper.

❧❦

Eye witness accounts lacked consistency. That was probably because the Ripper operated at night and in the shadows, and also because such was the hysteria around the Ripper's actions that many witnesses were not witnesses at all, instead just people wanting in the smallest way to be seen as a part of the biggest story in London.

❧❦

However, such patterns as emerge from their descriptions suggest the following: the Ripper was of average height and build, aged around thirty and of fair complexion. Barnett was 5' 7" tall, about average for the time, he was fair skinned and aged 30. Witnesses also described the Ripper as having a mustache (which was hardly unusual in the 1880s); Barnett too was mustachioed.

❧❦

Further evidence came from a letter allegedly sent from the Ripper, which claims to have

> 'saved some of the proper red stuff (blood?) in a ginger beer bottle.'

Some such bottles were found in the room at 13 Miller's Court occupied by Barnett at the time. However, given that the letter was most probably inauthentic, and possession of ginger beer bottles was not a crime, this evidence is hardly conclusive.

❧❦

Mary Kelly was the Ripper's final victim. Could it be that he no longer needed to kill if the reason for his crime spree was now dead?

One matter that was of great interest to the police was that the room in which Mary Kelly's body was found was locked. A reason for this could be that the killer possessed a key to the room; if so, Barnett would become a major suspect. But, equally, the killer could have exited through a window and reached back in to lock the door.

When the FBI released their profile in 1988, it could almost have been tailor-made for Joseph Barnett. A white male – tick; aged between 28 and 36 – another tick; living or working in Whitechapel – yes for both; absence of a father figure in childhood – his father died when he was very young; a job which allowed for the killer's violent tendencies – porters would cut and bonefish; the physical defect causing anger? Could that be his echolalia? Finally, Barnett must have known he would be a suspect in the eyes of the police – they interviewed him for four hours. That might have been enough to make him stop.

Altogether it is highly understandable that Bruce Paley should identify Barnett as being the Ripper. The case against him seems at the very least to be extremely strong. But there are other factors that need to be considered; Barnett had no history of extreme violence; he loved Mary Kelly; any evidence was circumstantial; the police at the time dismissed him as a suspect. Mind, this last point counts for little; police work back then consisted of little more than prejudiced guesswork. However, the above might add to the argument against Barnett being the Ripper. He was exactly the kind of man – of Irish heritage, drunken, unemployed, working class – whom the police would happily pin a crime if it were possible to do so.

❧

But he was released without charged and eventually remarried. He lived on until succumbing to edema of the lungs and bronchitis. He was sixty-eight years old.

❧

Before moving on to other suspects, there are two further points to consider. Firstly, was it possible that Barnett was not the Ripper, but still killed Mary Kelly, attempting to make it look like a Ripper crime? Or, might the police have held stronger suspicions towards Barnett but, like so many others, not want the killing to stop?

❧ IV ❧

A SUSPECT OF
CONVENIENCE

"There's nothing better than a little danger dashed with some romance."

— Kerri Maniscalco, Stalking Jack the Ripper

Taking a peek into our childhood past and remembering the TV horror shows about Jack the Ripper, or even characters loosely based on him, a picture forms in our minds. Top hat, long flowing cloak, his dark clothes. Digging deeper into those memories we see a face.

❦

It is the face of evil; one with dark, hooded eyes. Eyes that show neither empathy nor compassion. Thin eyebrows, not quite symmetrical, give a hint to the insanity breathing beneath them. We see angular features and high cheekbones. A mustache sits above the moody lips and beneath the prominent nose.

❦

We are looking into the face of Aaron Kosminski. For the authorities, the notion that Jack the Ripper was an immigrant, and a poor one at that, had many attractions. It drew attention away from the behavior of the rich who populated East End streets, looking for cheap sex to fulfill their seedy desires. It directed the anger of the indigenous East Ender towards a clear target; it even kept people off the streets (to some extent). For these authorities, which included the police, the idea that Jack the Ripper could be a Jewish immigrant was deeply appealing. Maybe they could keep up the pretense for months, even years. Murders based on a myth. In the end, criticism of their failure to find the Ripper changed their outlook, but by then the image was stuck. Take every caricature of the Eastern Jew and stick them under a top hat. The Ripper.

❦

Kosminski was a Polish Jew. He was born in 1965 (making him twenty-three at the time of the Ripper killing spree) in the town of Klodawa. Persecution by the controlling Government of the Russian Empire was an unpleasant fact of life for many Jews.

And also, like many, to seek an escape from that mistreatment, the Kosminski family decided to flee and set up a new life in the promised land of England, where the streets of London would be paved with gold. Or so they believed.

Instead, the Kosminskis left hell for purgatory; one persecuted community was replaced by another, once again they were aliens to the land, this time where a different language was spoken. Home became even more of a ghetto than it had in Poland.

By the time he was an adult, Aaron Kosminski was living with his two brothers and sister in Greenfield Street, which lay in the heart of Whitechapel. Records of the time are sparse, at best, and we know nothing about his parents. The future suspect had managed to find work and was a hairdresser in the district.

As we have seen, it suited the authorities to believe that Jack the Ripper was a Jew. Mass immigration into the East End of

London had turned a society already wary of Jews into one that was extremely anti-Semitic. So, it is not surprising to discover that the people who put Kosminski in the frame where two police officers.

⚜

Along with many others, Kosminski had been brought in for questioning at the time of the killings – after all, he was a Jewish man, so why not? There was, though, not an iota of evidence to link him to the crimes. Given that Victorians were not overly hot on absolute proof when it came to dishing out punishments to those they disliked, this suggests that there was no reason for bringing him in, other than his race.

⚜

And perhaps his behavior. Because three years after the Ripper's spree, Aaron Kosminski would be admitted to an insane asylum, following the wishes of his brother. This decision could be traced back to 1885 when Kosminski was just twenty. He suffered from auditory hallucinations – he heard voices. He also developed a paranoid fear of being fed by others. This led him to pick up food from the floor, to avoid getting his sustenance from the ministrations of others. Kosminski also developed a phobia about washing, which probably made having one's hair cut by him something of an ordeal. Indeed, shortly after his release from police investigations, he was admitted briefly to an institution, but left after three or four days. Unbeknown to him, the police were still following his movements.

⚜

By 1891 his mental health had deteriorated much more. He was firstly sent to the notorious Colney Hatch asylum in North London where if his diagnosis of being of '***unsound mind***' was not true at the time, then it soon would be. Then, in 1894 he was transferred to the Leavesden Asylum where he lived, if such a term can be used considering the conditions he would have been forced to endure, until his death from gangrene in 1919. It might be reasonable to conclude that Kominski's fifty-four years on earth did not offer the greatest of lives.

※

But none of the above is enough to see him launched into the top tier of suspects for being the true Jack the Ripper. So how did he enter such an undesirable group?

※

Sir Robert Anderson and Sir Donald Sutherland Swanson were senior police officers involved with the investigation. Given their lack of success in solving their biggest ever case, it might be a fair question to ask why they were given knighthoods?

※

Anderson's life was a catalog of failures. Brought up in a devout Christian home in Ireland, he rejected his faith before having a moment of enlightenment after listening to a sermon. It is worth noting that to progress in life during Victoria's reign a Christian calling card was an essential requirement. Living in his brother's shadow, he tried some careers before settling as a kind of political troubleshooter, although his lack of success suggested he was more trouble than shooter of it.

※

Anderson was deeply anti-Irish Republican and spent much of his life trying, and usually failing, to stop Fenian (the Irish freedom party) activities. When he was seconded to the Ripper inquiry, he felt it had been sensationalized and was firmly of the belief that the perpetrator had to be '*one of them*' rather than '*one of us*.' With no obvious Irish Catholic suspect, he presumably settled on the next best thing – a Polish Jew.

※

It's hard to understand quite what made simple Robert into Sir Robert, although he married into the establishment, which was probably enough.

※

Swanson, meanwhile, was the underwhelming leader of the Ripper inquiry. He made a career out of staying in the background and offering no controversial opinion on any matter unless completely unavoidable.

※

The only clues to his feelings on the Ripper inquiry he headed are that he believed the killer died after the fifth victim was murdered – which is a pretty convenient way of explaining why he had no suspect in custody. Later, he changed his opinion and named Kosminski as the likely killer.

He did so after reading that his great friend Anderson had offered that assertion.

⚬✺⚬

Truly, he did not come out directly with the Asylum inmate's name, instead stating that the killer was a '***Polish Jew***,' only later were his penciled notes found specifically identifying the immigrant.

⚬✺⚬

So, these were the men who put Kosminski into the frame.

⚬✺⚬

It is worth dwelling on Anderson's revelations because they offer an insight into the man. He released his memoirs in 2010, which were somewhat bizarrely entitled '***The Lighter Side of My Official Life***.' He goes on to talk about the Ripper case, and the Fenian investigations – it raises the question of what Anderson considered as the 'heavier' side of his life.

⚬✺⚬

He states the following:

> 'Undiscovered murders are rare in London...'

a point with which many would disagree,

> 'I am almost tempted to disclose the identity of the (Ripper) murderer, but no public benefit would

result from such a course. In saying that he was a polish Jew, I am merely stating an ascertained fact.'

Not that his memoirs were to become a best seller, but still Anderson manages to taint the entire Jewish religion with the unproven act of one man, then refuse to offer details of how he reached such a conclusion. Today we would call it racism.

Police did have a smidgeon of evidence that Kosminski might have been the killer. But it was tenuous in the least. And extremely confused. Only two witnesses' claims to have seen the Ripper have been given any credence. One was a Hungarian immigrant, Israel Schwartz who was believed to be Jewish himself. The Ripper was attacking Elizabeth Stride, his third victim, when Schwartz claims to have come across him. The attacker was startled and shouted an anti-Semitic insult at him. Schwartz got only the smallest glimpse of the attacker and then, fearing that he might be assaulted himself, made a getaway, Aaron Kosminski might have been many things but possessed of cunning wit was not one of them. The likelihood that he would have the speed of thought to imply he was not Jewish, by shouting an insult to Jews, is low.

The second witness was a cigarette salesman, Joseph Lawende. He was with two friends when he saw a man talking with Catherine Eddowes shortly before she was killed. Firstly, there is no certainty that the man was the Ripper. After all, Catherine was a prostitute, and talking with men was a regular occurrence for her. Secondly, Lawende also saw just a fleeting image of the man.

⚜

Anderson, though, used the alleged evidence of one of these to establish his theory of Kosminski's guilt. He claimed in his memoirs (odd that he should wait more than twenty years to do so) that one of the witnesses had identified Kosminski but would not testify because he was a fellow Jew.

⚜

Such a statement smacks more of anti-Semitism than fact, furthering the stereotype that the Jewish people stick together whatever the circumstances, even in the face of justice. The witness in question is generally believed to be Schwartz, who was at least Jewish. However, Anderson offers nothing firmer on which to base his assertion. It seems unsurprising that he was not a particularly successful investigator.

⚜

There is also the rather disconcerting fact that Schwartz's description bore little resemblance to Kosminski. The man seen was aged around 30 – Kosminski was only 23; he had a fair complexion, but Kosminski possessed swarthier features. The man described has a small mustache - Kosminski did have one of these – but so did most men of the time. However, his was bushy – it would certainly not fit in with his character to be a person who spent time manicuring his facial hair.

⚜

One other senior policeman would point the finger of accusation at Kosminski - a man of whom we will hear more later. Sir Melville Leslie Macnaghten was the Chief Constable of the Metropolitan police at the time the Ripper was active. He had nothing to do with the case at all. However, such a fact would rarely be seen as a reason not to seek a bit of attention for a certain breed of Victorian gentlemen. Macnaghten fitted this category.

◈

He reported that

> 'there were strong reasons for suspecting Kosminski because he "had a great hatred of women, with strong homicidal tendencies."'

Unfortunately, it seems that Macnaghten's grasp of little matters such as facts was as tenuous as his colleagues' Swanson and Anderson. There was no evidence at all to suggest that Kosminski hated women, and he did not show violent tendencies. It appears Macnaghten got his man confused with another Jewish inmate of an asylum, Aaron Cohen, who was violent.

◈

Still, they shared the same first name, which no doubt these gentlemen saw as enough cause for their suspicions.

◈

And so, the inclusion of Kominski in the list of chief suspects is something driven more by racial prejudice, and a desire to attach blame onto unwelcome immigrants, than anything based on fact. But then, in 2007, a new book appeared on the true crime shelves which (not for the first time) guaranteed to identify the Ripper.

⚜

Russell Edwards describes himself as an **'armchair detective**.' He is also heavily involved in the Ripper industry, operating tours of the killer's haunts. His book follows more than a decade of investigation and centers around a piece of clothing.

⚜

Let us start with the facts, as claimed, and then we will examine the probability of Edwards' beliefs being true. In the early hours of the morning of 30th September 1888, Police Constable Watkins discovered the mutilated remains of Catherine Eddowes. Laying close by was a scarf.

⚜

At the mortuary, Sergeant Amos Simpson made a grisly request, asking that he could take the shawl home – his wife was a dressmaker and would welcome the bloodstained material. Bizarrely, the request was agreed (who needs evidence in a murder inquiry?) but Mrs. Simpson was not impressed with her husband's re-cycling skills. She stored the shawl in a box (no doubt while wondering what sort of treats her husband might have in store for her at Christmas – a dead woman's teeth? A wig made from the hair of a murder victim?).

⚜

The shawl stayed in the family for generations, being handed down to a grateful relative after thankful offspring until it reached the possession of Sergeant Simpson's descendant, David Melville Hayes. In 1991, he handed it on to the Crime Museum at Scotland Yard. But ten years later, he took it back and displayed it at a Ripper conference.

⚙⚙

Then, it came up at an auction and Edwards, who had been searching for years for the one gem that could make his theories look credible, bought it. Thorough research led him to believe that the shawl had come from Eastern Europe in the early 1800s. The design led him to believe that the shawl was, in fact, not from the unfortunate Catherine Eddowes, but was instead a property of the Ripper.

⚙⚙

He engaged an expert in historic DNA testing, John Moore's University's Dr. Jari Louhelainen. As well as lecturing, Dr. Louhelainen had worked from time as an expert analyst in cold case investigations.

⚙⚙

The good doctor employed a new technique on the shawl, which allowed him to '*suck*' DNA from the garment. Then, testing against volunteer relatives' DNA, he made some incriminating finds.

- Blood on the shawl was deep, arterial blood.
  Catherine Eddowes had been savagely slashed with a knife and would bleed such blood.

- Kidney cells were discovered; Eddowes' kidney had been removed by her attacker.
- It was possible to extract mitochondrial DNA, which is passed down the female line and survives for longer than standard genomic DNA. This was found to be a 100% match to Catherine Eddowes' great, great, great granddaughter.
- The shawl contained semen stains.

One of his volunteers was descendent of Kosminski's sister, and a strong match was discovered between her DNA and the DNA found on the shawl. To Edwards, his case was proved. The scarf had been present when Eddowes was murdered. It contained both her and Kosminski's DNA. Therefore, Kosminski was the murderer.

෮෮෮

But as always with Ripper related matters, things are not quite that simple. Edwards' methodology has been questioned by many Ripperologists. He went to print extremely quickly after receiving the DNA information before his findings could be verified by a third party. His story generated significant media interest, with all the potential financial benefits that might bring.

෮෮෮

However, even if Edwards' methods might not stand the scrutiny of a proper forensic analysis, that doesn't mean that they are not correct. Which leads us neatly to examining the reliability of the conclusions he draws from the testing he had carried out on the scarf.

Dr. Louhelainen readily admits that he used a new method of DNA collection to make his findings. These involved soaking the shawl in a liquid and vacuuming up the resultant goo; he then separated the DNA from other materials he had taken up, and finally analyzed that DNA. New methods take a while to become established, and in the experimental stage, their findings are not always reliable. In this case, Dr. Louhelainen not only had to prove that the scarf contained blood from Catherine Eddowes but secondly tie Kosminski to it. That leaves a lot of room for error.

The DNA on the scarf must also have been contaminated. It had been passed through many hands − even Edwards was photographed touching it without gloves. It seems astonishing that in more than a century it had never been washed. Perhaps it had. Would the DNA evidence stand up in a court of law? In this case, almost certainly not. A half decent lawyer would tear the findings to shreds.

Nevertheless, for a moment let us assume that the blood does belong to Catherine Eddowes, and the semen stains to Aaron Kosminski − the second of these assertions being by far the less reliable of the two.

Who is to say that the two had not met anyway? Eddowes was a prostitute, and Kosminski would have been far from abnormal if he had made use of a prostitute's services. He may even had done so the night that she was killed. That is a supposition that we can now never prove...or disprove.

۞

Another consideration is that the shawl belonged to neither Kosminski nor Eddowes. It is possible that one or the other came across it, perhaps lying in the street, and took it for their own. Certainly, there is no evidence in any reports that Kosminski owned such a scarf.

۞

When we consider the 19th Century police's actions, we begin to see how tenuous a piece of evidence the scarf might be. These police did not even decide to hold on to it in the hope that somebody might identify it as belonging to either victim or aggressor.

۞

Despite the considerable limitations of the investigation, especially with Swanson in charge, they were still police officers, and presumably had at least some level of competence. They were quite happy for it the scarf be cut into some new piece of clothing by Amos' wife. Surely, they would not have allowed this if they believed the scarf was significant?

۞

Finally, there is the very fact that the scarf was left behind. In other attacks, the Ripper left no evidence beyond the body he had killed and mutilated. Of course, he was disturbed in attacking Catherine Eddowes, and therefore his modus operandi may have changed, but it still seems strange that he would be careless on this occasion.

⊗⅏⅏

This is a point that leads us towards two further considerations which lean towards Kosminski's innocence. Firstly, did he have the mental wherewithal to be so meticulous in his planning and operation? Almost certainly, not. Secondly, it is sometimes suggested that the scarf was a plant, one belonging to another individual entirely which was left to lead police towards an innocent person. If so, then again, the idea that Kosminski could plan and carry out such a ruse is highly unlikely.

ALREADY A SERIAL KILLER –
GEORGE CHAPMAN

Kosminski was not the only Jew to fall under suspicion. George Chapman had just arrived in England from his Polish home when the Ripper started his campaign – something which might lend credence to claims made against him. He had been born Severin Antoniovih Klosowski in 1865, making him just 23 at the time of the murders.

That, of course, sees him fall below the age range of the Ripper identified by the FBI. Chapman took numerous mistresses during his life...and often they ended up dead. He was suspected of killing at least three. It was only after the third of these, Maud Marsh, was exhumed that he was successfully tried and executed for her murder. This was in 1903.

That led newspapers to speculate that he may well have been the Ripper. However, beyond his location (he lived in the Whitechapel area in 1888) and that he murdered another woman, there is no further evidence linking him to the Ripper killings. He was not a suspect at the time and his method of murdering was poison rather than mutilation.

It seems more likely that suspicion fell on him because of his race rather than the likelihood of him being the killer. Racism takes generations to wear away!

❧ V ❧

THE ARISTOCRATIC
CONNECTION

"Wield your assets like a blade, Cousin. No man has invented a corset for our brains. Let them think they rule the world. It's a queen who sits on that throne. Never forget that."

— Kerri Maniscalco, Stalking Jack the Ripper

❦

As we will see later, it suited the politically liberal minority to raise the idea that the Ripper was some kind of villainous aristocrat, corrupted industrialist or educated professional gone bad. Thus, the poor of the East End became victims, pray for those with connections and a particularly unpleasant vice. Knowledge of their plight was raised.

❦

This viewpoint was one used to make a social point. But, while the convenience of laying the blame on the grubby hands of the Jew, Kosminski, was politically expedient, it didn't mean that the killer wasn't a Jew. Similarly, enabling a picture to be created of a society riven with exploitation did not exclude the Ripper being from the middle or aristocratic class.

A KILLER WHO COULD NEVER BE EXPOSED

❦

The Ripper was never identified. He killed five times in quick succession. Maybe more. He operated in an overcrowded part of London, and his story provoked widespread interest. His identity was never discovered. How? Good luck? Police incompetence? Both are possibilities. But an alternative theory for the Ripper remaining unidentified exists – an enormous establishment cover-up?

❦

While all three suspects named in this chapter had the money, contacts, and power to cover their tracks, more than any other, one kind of person would never be identified. A royal.

❦

Every time the idea that Prince Victor Albert is mentioned as being the Ripper, a chorus of disapproval meets the claim. However, there are general points to be considered: we know that the Prince did like to mix with prostitutes. Growing up in such a stultifying regime as he endured could well have contributed to this trait.

⚜

The theory most commonly put forward is that the Prince caught syphilis from a prostitute and the condition led to a mental breakdown, one for which he blamed prostitutes. Such was his anger at these sex workers that he took to the streets to attack and mutilate them.

⚜

The problem with this theory had always been that there was no evidence for the Prince contracting any variety of STI. Then again, such a condition for a royal, one who might even ascend to the throne one day, would be kept secret. But then, in 2015 some letters purportedly written by the Prince to his surgeon came to light. They had been kept in a private collection for years, but now appeared in an auction.

⚜

In one letter, written to '***Roche***' – we presume his surgeon – he asks for capsules to deal with his '***glete.***' He states that his '***glete***' is improving, now just appearing occasionally after a night's sleep. '***Glete***' is the name of a discharge that is a symptom of gonorrhea.

⚜

So, it seems that the Prince did suffer from an STI – most probably caught by a prostitute. However, that is the extent of the evidence against the Prince – there is nothing linking him directly to either the Ripper killings or even Whitechapel. He did not fit the description of the killer, and it is claimed that he was in Scotland during the Autumn of 1888. However, this would be a simple alibi to concoct for an institution as powerful as the palace.

We conclude that the likelihood that Prince Albert Victor was Jack the Ripper is negligible.

But the conspiracy does not end there. Another theory, believed to have come to light in the 1960s, is worthy of note in passing. This one states that the Prince had met, married and fathered a child with a young Catholic woman living in Whitechapel.

The notion of Catholic and Protestant blood mixing was probably a cause of greater royal angst than the idea that the heir but one to the throne should have a lover from a different class. After all, both his grandfather, Prince Albert, and his father, the soon to be King Edward VII were believed to have enjoyed playing the field. Particularly, the muddy fields populated by the lower classes.

However, goes the story, the Palace were afraid that the truth might come out, and as a result, three palace officers were deployed to kill anybody who might know about the scandal. The story does not hold much water – not least the question as to why the murders were so violent if they did not wish to attract attention. Nevertheless, it is a good example of how the Ripper killings continued to hold the public's attention throughout more modern times.

MAN ON A STICKY WICKET

꧁꧂

It is now time to return once more to the meandering accusations of Macnaghten.

꧁꧂

Montague John Druitt was, as his name suggests, of wealthy heritage; a member of the upper middle class so aspired towards by Victorians, not of royal blood. His father was a doctor, a highly regarded one at that, and young Monty enjoyed a privileged education, first at Winchester College and then Oxford University.

꧁꧂

Montague certainly had a troubled time, despite the good fortune of his birth, and we shall return to this later, but firstly, why would the mighty Macnaghten make a man such as Druitt one of his chief suspects? After all, if ever there was a class to which Macnaghten belonged, it was the one to which included Druitt. And one did not rat on one's peers.

⚜

But Macnaghten did... referring to the Ripper, the police chief asserted:

> 'The truth, however, will never be known and did
>   indeed at one time lie at the bottom of the
>   Thames, if my conjecture be known.'

⚜

In other words, as we shall see, the killer was, in Macnaughten's extremely humble opinion, Montague John Druitt. And the reason for this accusation? To the former Inspector, Druitt was the worst kind of man, one who had betrayed his kind. Because he was, to quote reports of the time, '***sexually insane***'; in other words, homosexual. Homosexuality was illegal between men yet was widespread and acceptable provided nobody knew about it. Interestingly, lesbianism was not a crime, because Queen Victoria had decreed sex between women was not physically possible. It was also seen as something associated with the French – and to Victorian Britons, things rarely got worse than that.

⚜

After university, Druitt made an unusual career choice. He spent some time as a Junior Master in a public school in Blackheath. But decided to enter the bar later. Fair enough, it may seem. But Druitt made the decision to continue with his work as a teacher as well as working as a lawyer. Despite his comfortable background, Druitt did need a salary to maintain his lifestyle – when his father died the sum he left was reasonable enough, it was just that little of it went to his two sons.

❦

Druitt was a keen and talented sportsman – something that will play a part in the likelihood of him being a genuine suspect for the crimes. He played Fives – a kind of handball game associated with the public schools, especially Winchester (along with Rugby and Eton), cricket and hockey.

❦

But it is his dual career that is the cause of most consternation. Because not only is it strange that he continued his secondary career as an assistant Master, but he was dismissed from his role just before the start of the Ripper killings. No evidence as to why he was dismissed exists, but it is fair to assume it was for some kind of discretion – maybe molesting the boys or making improper advances to anyone from the Headmaster's daughter to the assistant sewing girl; perhaps even the handsome young gardener. Possibly his misdemeanor involved violence...however Macnaughten's description of Druitt as 'sexually insane' does imply some kind of homosexual activity was the most likely cause of his dismissal.

❦

While all kinds of indiscretions were borne by young people in Victorian schools, outright abuse was considered just not cricket, even though it was widespread as summer matches on village greens.

❦

Then, within a couple of weeks of the death of Mary Kelly, the final Ripper victim, Druitt disappeared. He was found on December 31st, 1888 floating in the Thames. His death was no accident; it was suicide. Each of his pockets contained four large stones, placed there to ensure he drowned.

❦

But is there any other evidence to place the killings at this young man's door? Apart from the rambling assertions of Macnaghten, very few and those, such as do exist, are circumstantial.

❦

Physically, Druitt fitted the description of the Ripper. At 31, he was about the age identified by witnesses (and the FBI profile). Like the Ripper, he was well dressed. He was around the right height, although of slim build whereas the Ripper was described as burly. However, this could have been an illusion created by his cape.

❦

Druitt also came from a family with a history of mental illness. His mother had been committed to an asylum, where she had recently died. His grandmother and great aunt had committed suicide, and his sister had attempted to do so.

❦

Finally, when Albert Backert, who was a leading member of

the Whitechapel Vigilance Committee, complained about lack of police progress, he was told by the authorities:

> 'The man in questions is dead. He was fished out of
>   the Thames two months ago, and it would only
>   cause pain to relatives if we said any more
>   than that.'

❧

A bold statement, but one which the police would, or could, not back up with evidence. And when we come to evidence, that which did exist pointed strongly against Druitt being the killer. Because he was not in London at the time. On the day of Annie Chapman's murder, he was playing cricket in Dorset. Only by the most remarkable and hasty train journey could he possibly have arrived in London barely in time to kill a prostitute.

❧

With regards to his suicide, some researchers have claimed that this was from guilt at killing his five victims. Far more likely, it was an inherited mental illness – Druitt's suicide note says that he fears he is going the way of his mother. Perhaps whatever disgrace had led to his dismissal from the Blackheath school had pushed an already unstable man over the edge.

❧

It would appeal to Victorian society to lay blame at a man like Druitt's door. It appeals as an appeasement to the Whitechapel working class because Druitt is a representative of society's elite. However, not the most exclusive part of that club, who should be regarded as beyond reproach. Further, Druitt was most probably homosexual – cause enough to merit guilt in the eyes of those upstanding patriarchs of Victoria,

෧෴෨

However, when it comes to evidence against Druitt, there is little. Compared to the FBI profile, he fits only the most general of characteristics – gender and age. Was Druitt the Ripper? Almost certainly not.

PORTRAIT OF THE ARTIST AS A KILLER – WALTER SICKERT

❧

Sickert is considered one of the most talented and creative artists of his day – that day being late Victorian. Not for him were misty images of the British countryside, hunters on horseback. Nor stiff portraits of people far less important than they thought they were.

❧

Sickert instead caught real life; his was the world of the music hall; he painted nudes when the human body was meant to be covered beneath spreading layers of tight clothing at least, until the dark alley beckoned.

❧

His art made Sickert unpopular, but not a suspect in the Ripper inquiry. It was not until the early 1970s that his appearance in Alan Moore's graphic novel, From Hell, put him into the picture.

⚜

Even then, he would not have been considered a serious suspect had not novelist Patricia Cornwall used her name and talent to make the case against him. She purchased no fewer than thirty-two of his paintings from which to draw evidence.

⚜

Cornwall is sure she has her man, and if he is not the actual killer, then he was the man behind many of the letters to police and press that circulated. But her case is weak, and there are far more likely candidates.

⚜

Three wealthy, influential people. Each fits the image of the Ripper as the gentleman turned bad. Add to them the strong evidence (the tools of his trade, his anatomical knowledge) that suggest he could be a doctor and the idea that the Ripper is not a native of the East End is strong. But it is not conclusive.

❧ VI ❧
MURDERS A PLENTY

"Pretend I am as capable as a man? Please, sir, do not value me so little!"

— Kerri Maniscalco, Stalking Jack the Ripper

None of our suspects so far have any kind of strong case against them. George Chapman apart, none was proven guilty of any kind of serious crime. That is not the case with regards to our next group of potential Rippers.

DUNDEE'S LAST EXECUTION –
WILLIAM BURY

❦

Returning to the FBI profile of Jack the Ripper, William Henry Bury provides as close a fit as any suspect. Bury was 29 at the time of murders, a white male living with his wife, whom he had recently married, in Whitechapel.

❦

He was orphaned while still a young child, so grew up without a father's influence; and if he was the Ripper, he stopped for two reasons – firstly, he moved out of London just after the final Ripper murder, and then he confessed to killing his wife.

❦

Therefore, it is quite clear that he had a violent nature and given that he confessed to the savage murder of Ellen Elliot, which meant the gallows were an inevitable outcome, he may well have had some psychological disorder.

⁂

Further, Ellen was a prostitute. But there are even more reasons to suspect Bury. It is known that he was a quick-tempered and drunken man. Examples of this litter his past. He was caught kneeling over his new wife, threatening her with a knife. He slept with a pen-knife under his pillow.

⁂

His marriage to Ellen was most probably one he wished to exploit. His wife had inherited six shares in a railway company from an aunt, worth the not inconsiderable sum of £600. Within six months of their marriage, she had sold them all. Then, in January 1889, Bury planned to move to Australia. He went as far as getting packaging boxes made, but in the end, chose Dundee instead. Ellen did not want to go and only agreed when Bury lied that he had secured employment there.

⁂

Bury was a habitual liar, stealing keys to a basement room they lived in by pretending to be a potential renter. When he killed Ellen, the method he used was extremely like the murder of the first Ripper victim, Mary Anne Nicholls. Was this a modus operandi, or an extremely clever attempt to prove his innocence of this murder by creating suspicion that Ellen was another Ripper victim?

⁂

Because when Bury confessed to police, his story was not straightforward – although it soon fell apart. Bury claimed that he had been drunk and woke to find that his wife had hung herself. Fearing that police would suspect he was Jack the Ripper, he had cut his wife's body up, and hidden it, rather than getting help. Then, overcome by grief, he had come to confess. But a quick examination of the body told the authorities that the cutting had occurred at the time of strangulation; Ellen's jewelry on Bury's person added to their suspicions.

❦

Of course, murdering his wife does not make Bury the Ripper, but there were additional suggestions that he was the man. Two pieces of graffiti had been discovered, written in chalk, implying that the Ripper lived in their Dundee basement. Police suspected that this was the work of a local child, but even more tellingly were words Ellen shared with local women.

❦

Coming so far north while fears for the Ripper were at their highest prompted interest in what life was like in Whitechapel at that time. Her responses?

'Jack the Ripper is quiet now,' and 'Jack the Ripper is
    taking a rest.'

Of course, she could not know that the killer would not strike again...unless she knew him.

❦

The case against Bury has weaknesses. Most significantly is the fact that he was never a serious suspect to police...then again, their record was hardly exemplary. Many Ripper specialists also believe that Bury simply copied the Ripper's technique of strangulation followed by mutilation, probably in an attempt to confuse the authorities.

⚙

Nevertheless, compared to many other of the names put forward, Bury appears to be a more plausible contender as Jack the Ripper.

THE ESCAPEE – THE TRAGIC CASE OF JAMES KELLY

❦

It is pretty well impossible to hold sympathy for the Ripper. But if James Kelly was that man, then perhaps we can find it in our hearts to find a trace of regret.

❦

Kelly suffered from severe mental illness, most probably paranoid schizophrenia. He was born as the illegitimate child of fifteen-year-old Sarah Kelly, was brought up by his grandmother, only discovering that she was not his birth mother when Sarah died. He had never met her.

❦

Kelly spent much of his life traveling, but it was while he was training as an upholsterer that the pleasures of paid for sex came to him. However, then he met Sarah Brider, and life changed.

❧

He fell madly in love with Sarah, and (at the outset at least) that feeling was reciprocated. He persuaded her parents that he was a right and proper suitor for the young lady but when it came to pre-marital sex, she was a virgin, and he only used to be with cheap prostitutes. The event was a failure, and Kelly blamed his lover, telling her that she had a physical deformity.

❧

It was the beginning of the end. On June 4th Kelly and Sarah do marry, but this is the last desperate step made to save their relationship. Kelly has contacted a venereal disease, is finding it hard to remain in steady employment and, most worryingly, is beginning to display more and more extreme mood swings. These are becoming increasingly violent and will feature a verbal or physical assault followed by deep regret.

❧

Before long, the inevitable happens. Kelly launches a paranoid attack on his wife and her mother. He stabs her in the neck, then loses control and forces the knife in deeper and deeper.

❧

He is immediately distraught by his actions and is charged with attempted murder. This soon turns to murder when Sarah dies. However, rather than face the gallows, his mental illness is diagnosed, and he is sentenced to life in Broadmoor. However, he escapes and heads once more across the

Atlantic. There then follows a bizarre sequence of events whereby Kelly hands himself into some foreign embassy, is shipped back to Britain for arrest, but the authorities fail to turn up to take him in.

⚜

As a result, between the years of 1886 and 1927 nobody is completely sure of Kelly's whereabouts. Eventually, in 1927, the dying man hands himself in once more to Broadmoor, where he remains until his death two years later.

⚜

Evidence linking Kelly to the Ripper is tenuous – it is believed, but far from certain, that he was living in Whitechapel at the time the Ripper was active. He may have held hatred of prostitutes based on the venereal disease he caught. In his confused state, he may have blamed prostitutes for creating the circumstances that led him to kill his beloved Sarah. He had a violent temper, and how he killed his wife was not remarkably dissimilar to the methods used by the Ripper. Those points are all no more than circumstantial.

⚜

James Kelly is almost certainly not Jack the Ripper. Perhaps that is a good thing.

THE VAGUEST SUSPECT –
FRANCIS TUMBLETY

❧

Tumblety was a Canadian con artist. Or maybe Irish. He was born in 1833 – or perhaps he wasn't. He was the youngest of eleven children. That at least seems fairly indisputable.

❧

He was described as

'dirty, awkward, ignorant, uncared for, good for nothing'

as a child. Given that, the fact he made a more than a decent living in later life is something which should reflect well on him. Unfortunately, that work was as a charlatan – Tumblety claimed to be an Indian Herb Doctor.

❧

He was living in the US at the time and moved to Canada where he promoted himself to the rank of qualified physician – specializing in abortion. Unfortunately, those he treated tended to end up dead.

🕮

It seemed as though Tumblety held a deep hatred of women. He once told an acquaintance that he would rather give him a '***dose of poison***' than have a woman in the house.

🕮

Following an unfortunate mix up with the assassination of Abraham Lincoln (all to do with the various aliases he used), he left for Europe, ending up in Liverpool. Here, he embarked on a homosexual relationship with Henry Hall Caine, who would later gain fame as a novelist, although Caine was only 21 at the time of their affair.

🕮

By the time he entered his mid-fifties, he was Scotland Yard's chief suspect for being the Ripper. He was even arrested for the Whitechapel murders. He had been in trouble with the police several times and had been arrested charged with soliciting offenses against men, plus assault. The charge swiftly increased in severity. Police believed that they had their man. Or did they? Was it just the case that Tumblety neatly fitted their prejudices?

🕮

Monied but not middle class or aristocratic; alien – if not American, his accent suggested otherwise; homosexual. Beyond that their evidence was as shaky as ever. A collection of wombs was discovered in his home, weird, but given he claimed to be a doctor specializing in abortion, not impossible. He *may* have been residing in the Whitechapel area at the time of the killings.

⁂

Tumblety was bailed and his trial set for December 10th. But he took the opportunity to flee back the US, via France. In New York, he was kept under police surveillance, but the authorities there had no legal means to arrest him. Interestingly, while Tumblety's situation promoted forests of newsprint and speculation in the States, the same was not the case in Britain, although some reports suggest that Scotland Yard sent a detective after him to New York.

⁂

Eventually, the pressure on Tumblety became too much, and he fled until interest waned in his story. He resurfaced in Rochester, where he lived in considerable comfort with his sister until his death in 1903.

⁂

In 1993 a letter emerged, known as the Littlechild letter. The letter was a response to journalist GR Sims questioning of Chief Inspector John Littlechild in 1913. In it, the reasons (listed above) for Tumblety being charged were made clear. While they may be stronger than in some other cases, nevertheless, they remain uncertain at best.

Rather as with Druitt, the authorities of the time would certainly have liked the Ripper to have been Tumblety – but evidence for this was simply not there.

THE FORGOTTEN ONES

"Death was not prejudiced by mortal things such as station or gender. It came for kings and queens and prostitutes alike, often leaving the living with regrets."

— Kerri Maniscalco, Stalking Jack the Ripper

❧

Some estimates put the number of Ripper suspects at over one hundred. They range from American actor Richard

Mansfield to the highly unlikely Dr. Thomas Neill Cream. Mansfield was performing in a new play, The Strange Case of Dr. Jekyll and Mr. Hyde, at the Lyceum in the West End. One audience member was so struck by the transformation of Mansfield as he twisted himself into the murderous Jekyll that he wrote to Scotland Yard.

※

The theatergoer attempted to convince the police that such a performance could only be based on fact and experience. Mansfield was the Ripper.

※

Dr. Thomas Neill Cream was just as unlikely a Ripper as Mansfield. Not a nice person, he was serving time in prison during 1888. But Jack the Ripper evokes such strong feelings that some have tried to say that he worked with a double, with one committing crimes while the other established an alibi, being behind bars. It seems a strange and painful kind of alibi.

※

But as the list of suspects becomes increasingly bizarre – we have not mentioned those such as James Maybrick, only linked to the crimes through a diary which the owner admitted he forged – we should not forget one important point.

※

Jack the Ripper is from long ago, and he has almost turned

from vicious serial killer to stuff of legend – albeit a dark, satanic legend. With legends, truth soon turns to fantasy. And we forget that he was a mass murderer. In the fascinating search for his identity, we begin to lose track of the most important people in his story. His victims.

THE FIRST – MARY ANN NICHOLS
31ST AUGUST 1888

❦

Mary Ann was known locally as Polly. She was a popular figure around Whitechapel and looked younger than her forty-four years. One of the attractions of Polly was that she kept herself to herself, a trait much admired among the street workers of East London.

❦

She was also known for her cleanliness. Despite being an alcoholic, her doctor at her post mortem remarked, with some obscurity, on the cleanliness of her thighs.

❦

Polly, a nee Walker, had married William Nichols in 1864, and when she died, she left behind five children ranging in age from 21 to just nine years old. However, Polly and William had separated for the last of many occasions in 1881. While

Polly took to providing her services to her paying customers, the children lived with their father.

⚜

Her already tough life went downhill once she parted from William for the last time. She lived with her father for a while but ended up in a succession of workhouses. At other times she slept rough. For a short time, she worked in service, writing to her father to tell her that she was happy and working for good people. However, she was dismissed following some theft.

⚜

From there she took lodgings in a cheap room in Thrawl Street, where for the price of a loaf of bread or glass of gin she prostituted herself for her clients.

⚜

On the night in question, she left The Frying Pan Public House just after midnight, returning to her lodgings. However, she had no money to pay for her bed for the night and was sent back into the streets. Completely drunk, she met a fellow prostitute at around 2.30 am. They chatted briefly, and according to Holland Polly headed off once more to look for a trade. She was last seen alive walking down the Whitechapel Road.

⚜

At 3.45 her body was spotted by a man heading to work. Charles Cross was walking along Buck's Row when he saw

Polly's body. He called for help, and Robert Paul joined him. There was some doubt as to whether the victim was already dead. Worried about being late for work, which could cost them their job, the two men covered up the victim to make her decent and went off in the hope of seeing a policeman as they continued their journey.

※

In the meantime, her body was discovered by other police officers, who called for a doctor. He pronounced Polly dead at the site, saying she had just died.

※

At her inquest, the following wounds were described. Polly had lost five teeth, and her tongue was cut. A bruise on her jaw gave reason to this. Her neck contained knife lacerations. Then, on her lower abdomen deep cuts ran across and down her abdomen. The wounds suggested a killer out of control. That would become worse as his tally of victims increased.

THE WOMAN OF NAMES – ANNIE
CHAPMAN 8TH SEPTEMBER 1888

৩%৩

A nnie Chapman was already dying when she was murdered. She was suffering from TB and possibly syphilis. But despite this, despite a fondness for a drink, Annie was not an alcoholic, and her friends described her as a steady-going woman.

৩%৩

Annie had married and separated. She had lived with her coachman husband in more desirable areas than Whitechapel – Brompton, Bayswater and Berkeley Square – later they moved to Windsor.

৩%৩

However, John Chapman was a heavy drinker, and their marriage ended, amicably enough, three or four years before her death.

❃

It was around this time that Annie began to adopt pseudonyms – she moved in with a sieve maker, known as John Sivvey, and became Annie Sivvey; sometimes this melded into Sievey and Siffey. She also had the nickname of Dark Annie, perhaps on account of her dark, wavy hair. At the time, Annie was receiving occasional alimony from John, but when this stopped following his death, John Sivvey moved on.

❃

It was then that Annie took to the only means she had left of making a living – the streets. Without the shelter of John Sivvey, and the income from her ex-husband, her crochet work and flower selling did not make her enough to survive on.

❃

In early September she had a nasty bruise on her temple, the result of a fight with Eliza Cooper, her rival for the attention of her new boyfriend, Stanley (who was known as '*the pensioner*,' due to his military background). But a talk with her friend Amelia Palmer indicates that there was more wrong with Annie that evening. When Amelia commented on her bruised face, the older woman opened her coat and pointed to her chest, stating that she was too ill to work that night, and might try to get to her sister's house to stay over. But she showed Amelia her new black bonnet, which she was sure would bring her luck.

❃

On the night of September 7th, Annie was struggling. Her illness was not easing, but prostitution was the only means she had of making enough money to shelter her.

❦

Then at 5.30 am Albert Cadosch went to use the outhouse in the yard of his home. He heard a woman shout '**No**' and then a bang against his back fence. Annie's body was discovered there half an hour later.

❦

Her face was swollen, the tongue especially. Her body was extremely mutilated, and her throat almost cut through. Her abdomen too was savaged, and it appeared as though the instrument responsible was a bayonet or small sword, or perhaps the sort of surgical equipment used by a doctor, most probably for post mortem work. Doctor George Bagster Phillips, who attended Annie's dead body, concluded that the killer had some idea of anatomy. There were plenty of clues. Her entire stomach was torn open; her intestines had been lifted from her body and placed on her shoulders. The killer had performed a savage hysterectomy on the woman but had done so efficiently. He had to know what he was doing. And, whoever the killer was, he had used his knife with dexterity.

❦

The killer had struck again, this time with even more savagery.

❦

Among Annie's meager possessions was her favorite item of clothing, one who had bought her so much joy when she had got it a few days before – a small black bonnet.

THE SWEDISH WOMAN –
ELIZABETH STRIDE 30TH
SEPTEMBER 1888

☙

E lizabeth was born to the north of Gothenburg but moved to London at the age of twenty-three. By this stage, she had already worked as a prostitute in her own country.

☙

Like Annie Chapman, she was well-liked for her quiet demeanor and willingness to help in a crisis. But also, like Annie, she enjoyed a drink, and her character changed under the influence, and she would become loud, aggressive and bawdy. When in London she was a regular visitor to the Thames Magistrates Court under charges of being drunk and disorderly.

☙

Then in 1869, she married John Stride, and together they set up a Coffee Shop in Chrisp Street, Poplar, East London. Things seemed to be going well, and they moved to larger premises where they could also live, but then sold the business (which included their home) in 1875.

It was then that matters started to go downhill, sinking fast. Princess Alice was a saloon ship that steamed the Thames, and in 1878 it collided with another steamer, the Bywell Castle. Seven hundred people died in the tragedy, including John, and Elizabeth was kicked in the face while trying to escape.

Except that probably was not true. John Stride survived for another six years, and there were no signs of injury to Elizabeth. Today, it is thought that she made her claims to get a payout from the Swedish Church in London.

After John Stride died – properly this time – Elizabeth spent time in the workhouse, but then entered a violent relationship with a laborer, Michael Kidney. Meanwhile, she took more and more heavily to drink and ended up in a lodging house.

It was there that she met Thomas Barnardo, of children's home fame. He was researching conditions in the East End and was visiting the lodging house. This uncertain life continued for Elizabeth for some time. She was by now forty-four years old and on September 30th entered the last day of her life.

❧

It was a busy one; by midnight she had already been seen with three men. The last of these was witnessed by a police officer and was carrying a parcel wrapped in newspaper. Although not shaped like a knife, it could well have contained one. However, within ten minutes Israel Schwartz witnessed and attempted to intervene in an attack on Elizabeth. He reported seeing a second man in the shadows, who might or might not be an accomplice.

❧

The description he gives, though, does not match the description provided by the policeman. It seems likely that the parcel carrier was not the Ripper.

❧

Some ten minutes later, Louis Diemschutz turned into Dutfield's Yard driving his pony and cart. He saw a hunched shape, which split into two when it was disturbed. One part ran off; the other was the dead body of Elizabeth Stride. Unless the unlikely event of two attacks had happened to her in the space of ten minutes, the Ripper was the man who had scared off Israel Schwartz.

❧

If his other victims suffered from enormous mutilation then

it was clear that Elizabeth had been spared that, for what comfort it is worth. Her throat was slashed, and there was bruising on her face and neck, but her abdomen was unharmed. It was clear that the Ripper had been disturbed and stopped in his tracks. Which, it would seem, was extremely bad news for his next victim.

THE RIPPER'S ACQUAINTANCE? – CATHERINE EDDOWES 30TH SEPTEMBER 1888

❧

While she was still a child, Catherine walked with her family from Wolverhampton to London as, Dick Wittington like, they sought their fortune. Alas, it was not to be found on the filthy streets of the capital. Her father headed back to the Midlands, while Catherine and her siblings stayed with their mother. But when she died, Catherine was sent to the workhouse. She was just thirteen years old.

❧

However, her aunt took her in, and she stayed there until she was twenty, when she ran off with Thomas Conway, a retired soldier. They had three children, although it seems that they never married. After they split, she entered a tumultuous relationship with John Kelly, who did odd jobs around the markets. Catherine, who was known as Kate (sometimes Kate

Kelly) was not the settling kind and would hop around the country, turning up here and there before usually returning to London for a few difficult weeks with John or her children.

※

But although she never had money, and even her daughter got fed up with her scrounging and hid herself away in Bermondsey, most people had a good word for Catherine. They said that she was always happy and sang a lot. She was a bright woman, and the only blot on her character seemed to be a vicious and unpredictable temper. Unlike most others in her position, she was rarely drunk.

※

Just before her death she returned to London again and found a bed in a lodging house where she was well known.

'I have come back to earn the reward offered for the apprehension of the Whitechapel murderer,'

she is alleged to have told the superintendent of the hostel, although presumably in a less formal way.

'I think I know him.'

Whether or not that was true, she would certainly meet him in a few days with devastating consequences.

※

On the afternoon of September 29th, she decided to head to

Bermondsey to see if she could get a few pennies from her daughter. That failed because the daughter had moved again to avoid her scrounging mother. By the early evening, she was to be found in Aldgate, midway between the East and West Ends of London, unusually for her, drunk. By 1.00am the police discovered that she had sobered up and allowed her out of her cell.

❦

Within the hour she was discovered dead. The fourth victim.

❦

It seems as though being disturbed in his attack on Elizabeth Stride threw the Ripper into a frenzy. His mutilation of Catherine was by far the most extreme to date. Her throat was cut through, and her ear had been sliced, almost with care. Her torso was slashed down its length, and her intestines had been cut out and left over her shoulder. A section had been cut free and placed between her arm and body. Internally, there were wounds to her liver, and the Ripper had sliced through her vagina to her rectum. Her inner thighs had been mutilated. Her womb had been sliced from her body, and just a stump remained.

❦

When the body was examined more fully the surgeon discovered a section of Catherine's ear caught in her clothing. Once washed, he could see that her face had been cut, almost as though the Ripper was trying to remove her eyes. The tip of her nose was almost sliced through. Further cuts had torn open her cheeks and upper lip.

The surgeon, Dr. Frederick Brown, decided that death had been instant the moment her throat was cut, and the mutilation had followed post mortem.

THE LAST VICTIM? – MARY JANE
KELLY 30TH 9TH NOVEMBER 1888

☙❧

We have already come across Mary Jane Kelly and her relationship with Joseph Barnett. Mary was just twenty-five when she died, younger than all the other victims.

☙❧

Other than acquaintances saying she was a quiet, attractive girl who changed when the liquor flowed too readily, all that we know about Mary came from Joseph Barnett – the extent to which that can be trusted is open to question.

☙❧

It seems as though she grew up in Wales, perhaps Carnarvon and later Cardiff, and arrived in London when she was twenty-one. Equally, she may well have held Irish connections, because the landlord at one of the hostels in the East

End said that she once received a letter from her mother there.

⁂

Mary was discovered in her room at the lodging house in Miller's court at 10.45 in the morning. The last sitting of her had been in the early hours when she was witnessed with a flamboyantly dressed man about ten years her senior. The witness described him as looking Jewish. When the papers reported this, they changed the man's description to make this suspect dark-haired and swarthy, rather than sandy-haired and with a pale complexion. Nothing being too serious for a stereotype in those days, it seemed. Or maybe there was another reason for the misreporting. The proper description of this man fits in with that of the Ripper, the one reported does not. Was it that the press, in collaboration with other authorities, were keen for the Ripper story to continue and not end with the man's capture?

⁂

But whether this man was the Ripper, we do not know. One of the biggest differences with Mary Kelly's death compared to the others was that she was murdered indoors. Had the Ripper decided that he could enjoy more time and safety if he took his victims to their homes? Once there, he could mutilate at will with little chance of discovery. However, it could also be the case that Mary's death was a copycat killing. According to Macnaghten, she is one of the five official victims, but as we have already seen, the words of this police officer have to be taken with a large pinch of condiment.

⁂

Nevertheless, the pattern of ever-growing mutilation was consistent with Mary's murder. Her entire abdominal cavity had been opened and cleared. Her internal organs were found scattered around the room. Her thighs had been skinned, and her breasts cut off. One was found under her bed. Her legs had been stripped of their skins to her knees, and he had slashed her lower legs and arms.

⚅⚅

The killer had hacked her face until she was unrecognizable, and her neck had been cut using such force that her head was almost separated from her neck. The murderer had removed her heart.

⚅⚅

The Ripper industry today is built on entertainment. When we think back to the reality and viciousness of his attacks, that industry looks increasingly inappropriate. It makes us question whether the thrill and shivers we feel when we consider this man are exploitation of his victims. Today, he exists as an almost mythical person, in 1888 he was very, very real.

THE LIST GOES ON

❦

The five detailed above are those usually considered as definite victims of the Ripper. They are called canonical victims. The basis for this judgment is, though, based on the rambling observations of Macnaghten. For that reason, we must consider that there could have been more, or even fewer, victims.

❦

Numerous other attacks could well have been committed by the man. Even more are copycat crimes, where the subjects have been attacked as though the Ripper were responsible.

❦

Of the more prominent assaults to fit into these two categories are:

❦

Fairy Fay – the first potential Ripper victim, who is alleged to have been murdered on Boxing night in 1887. Little is known of Fairy Fay, and most experts believe she was neither murdered nor, possibly, ever existed.

❦

Martha Tabrum – if Fairy Fay was probably fictional, then Martha was certainly not. It appears as though she was raped and murdered on August 7th, 1888. She was killed by stabbing and could well have been the early casualty whose death led to ever more serious mutilations later. However, she had last been seen with a soldier, and no Ripper descriptions suggest a military connection.

❦

Rose Mylett was murdered on December 20th, 1888. Ripper news had fallen flat, and public interest seemed to have dimmed by this time. However, in some ways, Rose was a classic victim. She was killed just a couple of miles from Whitechapel – had the Ripper extended his field? Perhaps he felt increasingly vulnerable in his traditional home. It appeared as though she had been strangled from behind. Since his motivation for murders seemed, in part, to be the mutilations he carried out post mortem, maybe the Ripper was trying new methods to kill his victims quickly and silently.

❦

Rose was both a prostitute and a drunk. As such, she merited little attention from the authorities. Interest in the Ripper was on the wane. The police did little to pursue the crime, even suggesting it might have been suicide. However, Dr. George Baxter Phillips gave evidence at the inquest into her death and pointed out the similarities with the murder of Annie Chapman in particular. The doctors who had carried out the post mortem also believed foul play was responsible for her death. The jury agreed.

※

The police though had no wish to expose themselves once more to criticism for failing to catch the Ripper. They refused to investigate Rose's case. They may have missed another victim.

※

And so, the list continues, with greater or lesser conviction. Other potential prey includes Elizabeth Jackson, Alice Mackenzie, Annie Smith, Frances Coles...until we reach **Carrie Brown**, who died on April 24th, 1991.

※

But not in London, or even the UK. Carrie was a friendly, older prostitute who lived in New York. The link which tied her death to the Ripper killings was that she was gutted after being murdered. Her killer was never found, and almost certainly was not the Ripper himself. Carrie was the last credible person to be considered a victim of the Whitechapel murderer.

❧ VIII ❧
THE MAKING OF A MURDERER

"Monsters were supposed to be scary and ugly. They weren't supposed to hide behind friendly smiles and well-trimmed hair. Goodness, twisted as it might be, was not meant to be locked away in an icy heart and anxious exterior."

— Kerri Maniscalco, Stalking Jack the Ripper

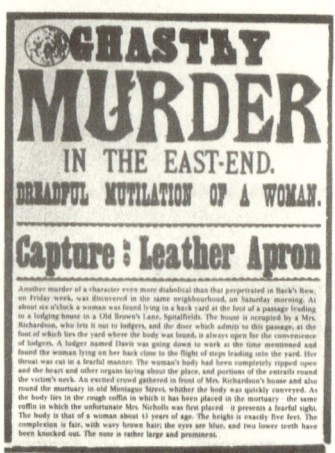

The FBI profile mentioned earlier offers as close a picture of the killer as we will probably ever find. But unless we ever discover his name, any conclusions we draw are pure conjecture.

Something led to this man entering our culture. Partly, that is the gruesomeness of his crimes. Still, to Victorians, his victims were mere prostitutes and as such people not worthy of the level of attention they received. Something lifted this killer to the status of a bogeyman, to the legend of one who haunts the dead of night. Still. After more than a century. Something kept that picture alive, decades after the real Ripper must have died.

The conduit to his enduring legacy was the media, specifically the Pall Mall Gazette. Initially, that paper was simply another Times or Telegraph, a voice piece for the establishment. Consider the anti-Jewish sentiments we saw from it earlier. Then, in 1880 a young assistant editor was appointed. Hailing from Northumberland, and the son of a farmer, William Thomas Stead was anything, but the public school educated, aspiring aristocrat of his peers. And when he became full editor three years later, he took the traditionally conservative paper down a different path. A long, rocky and sometimes risky path close to the cliff edge that was life under Victoria.

※

Stead saw through the thin veneer of Victorian society. He could see the smoldering corruption that was barely hidden by the velvet curtains of good grace and name. And he wanted to expose it.

※

The Pall Mall Gazette switched its alliances to the more socially reformist Liberal Party and made its first target for exposure child prostitution. At the time, the age of consent for girls was just 13. (There being no age of consent for boys in no way lessened abuse for many male youngsters). Thanks to work by Stead in exposing the contradictions in a supposedly moral society that allowed men to have sex with thirteen-year-old girls, the age of consent was raised to sixteen.

※

But this came at a cost to the newspaper editor. No doubt, there were many in the corridors of power and the clubs of St James who saw the prospect of their secret peccadilloes becoming illegal. Stead was fitted up with a charge of securing child prostitution and convicted on a technicality. He had investigated the horror by paying five pounds to buy a girl and then encouraged her to tell her story. He had done nothing more than reveal the truth. Nevertheless, rich society's mores were challenged, and he was charged with failing to inform the girl's father of his actions. The three-month sentence he received backfired on the establishment, making the Gazette more popular than ever and allowing its views to infiltrate far greater swathes of society who had doubts about the way things were run.

৪৯৪

So when the Ripper story broke, steadily, over August and September 1888, Stead was appalled by the coverage. Cartoon papers such as the Police news presented the killings as a kind of darkly humorous story. Caricatured, swarthy hunch-backs – Jewish features to the fore – were cast as villains as they attacked comic book prostitutes, wearing remarkably clean clothing.

৪৯৪

Even more worrying to Stead were the presentations of the establishment press, whose influence was designed to rein-force the status quo. Here, the East End was to blame for its suffering, having allowed vicious immigrants to dirty its streets. The area was full of drunks and prostitutes – a different world to the genteel homes of their readership. As such, it was as though the murders were taking place in some dusty foreign land, rather than three miles from parliament.

৪৯৪

Stead put paid to that. In a series of reports and articles, he exposed the reality of life in the East End. He brought to public attention the unbelievably harsh levels of poverty, the powder keg that existed between natives and the growing immigrant population and, most painfully of all; he told the truth about the role of rich Victorians and East End Music halls.

⚜

In one article, published in mid-September 1888, his paper openly tells its readership to look beyond the caricatured criminal type, with dirty skin and toothless mouth, like the killer in the Ripper case. It points out that many of the worst crimes over time have been committed by the educated and wealthy. It shows that behind the façade of gentility, countless rich industrialists, middle-class professionals, and sordid aristocrats use the East End as a cheap and secret way to satisfy their sexual desires.

⚜

It is easy to understand the shock that reverberated through the drawing rooms of London and beyond. And the anger. Letters flooded to both the Gazette and its rivals; many expressed outrages, some support. More offered random thoughts about the murders and one, famously, in claiming to be from the killer (it almost certainly wasn't) was signed, Jack the Ripper. The killer had an identity, and society was shaken up.

⚜

Such was the backlash that a year later Stead was forced to

resign his editorship, and the paper returned to its conservative roots before eventually disappearing altogether. Stead himself died on the Titanic, a death no doubt every bit as frightening as the demise of the East London prostitutes whose stories he told.

※※※

Whether or not the Ripper was a rich man – and the balance of probability remains that he was not – Stead and the Pall Mall Gazette achieved three major objectives in its campaign. It told the sheltered public that the East End was a real place, with real people living real, difficult, lives. It raised awareness of the duplicitous nature of a society whereby morals are public, and sins are private but widespread. And it raised the prospect that middle class and aristocratic people do fall to the depths of depravity shown by the Ripper.

※※※

Everybody loves the idea of privilege gone bad and allied with a name that stuck in people's minds; the legend was born.

❧ IX ❧
CONCLUSION

❦❦❦

Mostly, we can draw our lessons from a person's life; their biography offers insights, traits, and decisions that we can adapt to ourselves.

❦❦❦

Jack the Ripper, whoever he might be, offers no such benefits. A sociopath, a man with absolutely no empathy for his victims, he is one of the vilest humans in history.

❦❦❦

Whether rich man or poor, Briton or immigrant, this was a man who targeted his victims and killed with a coldness planned enough to ensure that his victims could not scream for help or fight back. More than lessons from the character of this man, whoever it might be, we can learn from society's response to him. Many of these learn are not good.

⚜

The fear and vigilante groups that sprang up in the East End are understandable. The police reaction, seeking to place the blame at the door of one of society's rejects is of its time, indefensible but explicable. However, the decision of senior officers to pick suspects on whims, using only the thinnest of evidence, is despicable. Perhaps, in a small way, the criticism leveled at the authorities led them to make the slightest of changes in their attitudes.

⚜

Perhaps they became a little more tolerant, a little more willing to base their conclusions on evidence rather than prejudice.

⚜

The man who comes out best from the Ripper debacle is John Stead. He used the developing story to highlight the corruption at the top of the supposedly immaculate Victorian society. He showed to the poor of Whitechapel that they did not need to accept exploitation by those with money and power. He bought the appalling East End conditions, like Charles Dickens before him, to the eyes of the nation. More than that, he helped to open those eyes.

⚜

The change was slow, and poverty existed in extreme proportions right up to the end of the second world war. The recent Greenfield Tower disaster, where poor upkeep and cheap materials contributed to the death of 72 Londoners, many of them poor immigrants, demonstrates that some of the inequalities of Victorian Society remain. However many politicians tell us that they don't.

⚜

Perhaps that is the biggest lesson we can draw – that we should always open our eyes to abuse, poverty, and exploitation, and whenever it is in our power to do so, be fearless in challenging them.

⚜

The establishment is strong and self-perpetuating. No doubt without people such as John Stead the iniquities of Victorian Britain would never have been challenged. Stead paid dearly for his exposures – imprisonment and losing his job. Nevertheless, he remains a social pioneer of his age.

⚜

But there is another side to Jack the Ripper. The story of his campaign of terror continues as strongly as ever. Yes, a part of that is the way we like to be titillated by fear, but because the Ripper was real, that titillation is based on truth, and when we think about the Ripper, our mind travels to the horrors of the 19th century East End. Evils occur less often when they stay in the public eye, whether the evils of the acts or, more importantly, the evils of the society that gives birth to them.

＊＊＊

Early in the book, we said that we would not identify the
Ripper, and in all likelihood, anybody that does claim to be
able to name the man is acting on pure conjecture.

＊＊＊

We have not identified him. Indeed, we have shown that it is
likely that none of the main suspects is the man. And that is
good, isn't it? Because the story of Jack the Ripper would not
endure if we knew who he was.

❦ X ❦
FURTHER READING

- Phil Sugden – The Complete History of Jack the Ripper – a comprehensive look at the case.
- Patricia Cornwall – Portrait of a Killer – Jack the Ripper: Case Closed – not especially authoritative but well written and, in its way, entertaining.
- Bruce Paley – Jack the Ripper: The Simple Truth – highly regarded by Ripper aficionados.

❦

Also worth a look...

❦

When in London, official Ripper Tours are easily found. Among the best is the Jack the Ripper Tour with '**_Ripper Vision_**.'

❦

Even better is the Jack the Ripper Museum, in Cable Street.

YOUR FREE EBOOK!

As a way of saying thank you for reading our book, we're offering you a free copy of the below eBook.

Happy Reading!